CW00725364

DARK HORSE
COMPANION
FLAT SEASON 2019

MARTEN JULIAN

Published in 2019 by Marten Julian
69 Highgate, Kendal, Cumbria LA9 4ED

Copyright © Marten Julian 2019

The right of Marten Julian to be identified as the author of this work has been asserted by him in accordance with the Copyright, Designs and Patents Act 1988.

All rights reserved. No part of this publication may be reproduced, stored in a retrieval system, or transmitted in any form or by any means, electronic, mechanical, photocopying, recording, or otherwise, without the prior written permission of the publishers.

A catalogue record for this book is available from the British Library.

ISBN 978-1-9998388-9-8

Cover design by Steve Dixon
Designed by Fiona Pike
Photographs supplied by the Racing Post

CONTENTS

INTRODUCTION 5

THE PREMIER LIST 7

THE DARK HORSES 17

THE DARK HANDICAPPERS 39

THE QIPCO 2,000 GUINEAS PREVIEW 51

THE INVESTEC DERBY PREVIEW 63

THE QIPCO 1,000 GUINEAS PREVIEW 73

THE INVESTEC OAKS PREVIEW 83

INDEX 87

The Weekend Card features news and weekly advice from a knowledgeable and informed team of writers. Headed by Marten Julian, who was established in 1970, not only does it focus on the main action over the course of the weekend, it also unearths unexposed talent and draws your attention to horses with the potential to improve.

It isn't just about the weekend. The Weekend Card can be referred to throughout the season as it offers long-term advices including ante-post selections

Past copies are available to view online or by calling us and requesting a **free information pack.**

THE ETHOS OF THE WEEKEND CARD IS CONTINUITY

With this in mind this publication is the only place where you can read weekly news on horses that feature in Marten's publications.

SUBSCRIPTION OPTIONS

Posted First Class each Thursday / Posted First Class each Thursday with a complimentary email copy / Download it through our website on the weeks you want it.

5 Issues £30: 10 Issues £55: 20 Issues £100

WEEKLY RACING INFORMATION

Packed with over 5000 words of thought-provoking content, for as little as £5 per wee

Contact details: 01539 741 007

rebecca@martenjulian.com / www.martenjulian.com

INTRODUCTION

Thank you for buying this 2019 edition of the *Dark Horse Companion*.

I hope that you find the book a useful source of reference and enjoyment through the course of the season. If you are buying the book for the first time here is a brief guide to how the horses have been selected.

My qualifiers for the Premier List are chosen in the expectation that they will have rewarded support to level stakes by the end of the season. It is my belief that they possess the attributes to merit our special interest and attention.

The selections for the Dark Horses feature are generally more lightly raced, unexposed or unraced – most of them with a long-term future.

The Dark Handicappers are, as indicated in the title, unexposed horses that I believe were campaigned last season with handicaps in mind.

Please note that with respect to the Classic Previews, the entries for the Oaks were not available by the deadline for the book.

You can be kept updated with my latest thoughts on the horses featured in this book either through my *Weekend Card*, which monitors the progress of the Premier List horses every week, or by ringing my line, which is updated every day (0906 150 1555).

For further details of a subscription or text-based service please ring Rebecca (01539 741007) or contact her by email (rebecca@ martenjulian.com).

I am, as always, indebted to Rebecca, James Norris, Ian Greensill, Jodie Standing, Steve Dixon, Paul Day and Fiona Pike for their help at various stages of the production.

Finally, I would like to wish you the very best of good fortune for the season.

Bye for now.

Marten

THE PREMIER LIST

The following horses have been selected in the expectation that they will reward support through the course of the season.

ALL POINTS WEST (3YR BAY GELDING)

TRAINER:	Sir Mark Prescott
PEDIGREE:	Speightstown – Albamara (Galileo)
OPTIMUM TRIP:	1m 2f +
FORM:	000 –
RATING:	68

Second foal out of Listed-placed daughter of Galileo who stayed middle distances from the family of Group 3 winner Algometer and 2m 3f winner Alwilda.

Shaped quite well last season, notably on his second start at Kempton where he was shuffled along to finish seventh, staying on steadily to the line and beyond. Slowly away next time in a 7f novice event at Chelmsford, again keeping on quite well towards the finish.

Not badly treated on 68 taking lines through Buffalo River and Ajrar, rated 89 and 94 at the time of their Kempton form. Will stay 1m 2f and bred to get further. Very interesting.

ALMANIA (3YR BAY COLT)

TRAINER:	Sir Michael Stoute
PEDIGREE:	Australia – Sent From Heaven (Footstepsinthesand)
OPTIMUM TRIP:	1m +
FORM:	41 –

Cost 500,000gns as a yearling and the third foal of Group 3-winning half-sister to 1m 2f Group 3 winner Above Average and middle-distance winner Granddukeoftuscany.

Shaped reasonably well when fourth in a fair 6f maiden at Ascot in July, keeping on at one pace in the final furlong.

Ran a remarkable race in a 7f Class 5 maiden at Sandown next time, up there handy and leading two furlongs out only to look beaten when headed by Buffalo River entering the final furlong before battling back to regain the lead in the closing stages.

Displayed great tenacity up the hill, with the first two drawing seven lengths clear of the third. Runner-up now rated 89, with subsequent winners in third, now rated 89, sixth and last.

Trainer seldom far adrift in his assessment of a horse's ability and reports suggest he rates this colt highly. May appreciate a mile and quick ground.

CHANCER (3YR BAY GELDING)

TRAINER:	Sir Mark Prescott
PEDIGREE:	Lope De Vega – Misk (Linamix)
OPTIMUM TRIP:	1m 4f +
FORM:	000 –
RATING:	62

Sixth foal and half-brother to winners at up to 1m 6f out of a middle-distance winning half-sister to 1m 4f Listed winner Mashoor.

Did not show obvious promise on his first two starts but ran much better on his final outing in a 7f maiden at Doncaster, travelling well through the first half of the race until appearing to tire in the final quarter-mile, finishing seventh of 13.

Did well to show such pace given the very strong bias towards stamina in the bottom half of his pedigree. Likely to thrive for his astute handler and could progress into a useful staying handicapper by the autumn.

EVEN KEEL (3YR CHESTNUT COLT)

TRAINER:	Jonathan Portman
PEDIGREE:	Born To Sea – Dew (Whipper)
OPTIMUM TRIP:	1m
FORM:	22201312 –
RATING:	94

First foal of a half-sister to 10 winners including Solid Approach, a winner up to 1m 4f, Zero Money, Dangle and Bahati – all winners at up to 7f.

Appears thoroughly exposed on first sight, having run eight times last season and risen from a mark of 76 to 94, but has displayed admirable tenacity in his races and could progress still further.

Ran second in auction races on his first three starts and fifth from an opening mark of 76 on his nursery debut before winning a 7f nursery at Newbury off 75. A gutsy third next time at Sandown off 80 was followed by a tough front-running display from a mark of 83 over a mile at Newmarket before a narrow defeat off 91 in a 1m nursery at York.

Has shown his form on both good to firm and soft ground, but thought by his trainer to favour ease underfoot. May stay beyond a mile but doesn't need to. Already on the cusp of Listed class and has the ability and tenacity to make that next step. Admirably tough and very well handled by his trainer.

GREAT MIDGE (4YR BAY GELDING)

TRAINER:	Henry Candy
PEDIGREE:	Kyllachy – Super Midge (Royal Applause)
OPTIMUM TRIP:	5f +
FORM:	0224 –
RATING:	75

Fourth foal and full brother to 6f AW winner Fivetwoeight and half-brother to winners over 5f and 6f. Dam full sister to 6f Group 3 winner Tremar from a very speedy family.

Lightly raced maiden who has shaped well, notably when runner-up on his second and third starts at Doncaster and Salisbury, before luckless run on his handicap debut from a mark of 75 in 6f contest at Kempton, behind early from wide draw in stall 10 before quickening from the home turn to reach challenging position entering the final furlong. Could only run on at one pace close home to finish fourth.

Has shown he can win races from this mark and may be suited to a strongly run five furlongs. Still unexposed.

KADAR (3YR BAY COLT)

TRAINER:	Karl Burke
PEDIGREE:	Scat Daddy – Kaloura (Sinndar)
OPTIMUM TRIP:	1m 2f +
FORM:	1 –

€700,000 two-year-old purchase and the fifth foal of Listed middle-distance winning half-sister to Breeders' Cup Turf and Champion Stakes winner Kalanisi and 1m 2f Group 2 winner Kalaman.

Has long been held in high regard by his trainer and went a long way to justifying that reputation when displaying a commendably mature attitude to beat the useful Waldstern, now rated on 98, by a length and a quarter in a 1m novice stakes at Haydock in September.

Tracked leaders on the rails and pushed along two furlongs from home, was then switched and ran on well to win going away nicely at the line. Shaped as if this trip was his minimum requirement and may well prove effective at a mile and a half.

Sure to earn black type this season and has the physique and pedigree to progress with the passing of time. Enjoyed the easy ground and looked very tough at Haydock.

MATCHMAKING (4YR CHESTNUT GELDING)

TRAINER:	Sir Mark Prescott
PEDIGREE:	Mastercraftsman – Monami (Sholokhov)
OPTIMUM TRIP:	1m 4f +
FORM:	000/11113 –
RATING:	82

Second foal of a 1m 2f Group 2 winner (disqualified) half-sister to Italian Oaks and 1m 4f US Grade 2 winner Meridian.

Shaped with a modicum of promise in three starts at two and built on that from an opening mark of 60 when winning four on the trot over 1m 2f at Yarmouth (60), Brighton (66), Bath (69) and Wolverhampton (75) before appearing to be beaten on merit into third off 82 in an extended 1m 3f Class 5 handicap at Lingfield.

Tends to race on and off the bridle and still required plenty of nudging along on his final start. May not have been at home on the fast ground or the tight tracks at Brighton and Bath in the summer and entitled to improve for a step up in trip around a more galloping track.

Could be one to keep in mind for a valuable sponsored handicap, with the Ebor a possible target if his rating rises.

PLAY IT BY EAR (3YR CHESTNUT COLT)

TRAINER:	Iain Jardine
PEDIGREE:	Dragon Pulse – Seriously (Sinndar)
OPTIMUM TRIP:	1m 2f +
FORM:	OOO –
RATING:	67

Third foal of a half-sister to an Italian 1m 2f Group 3 winner and Italian Derby third.

Looks ideally poised to win handicaps, having caught the eye with a late flourish inside the final furlong on his debut in a 1m novice auction stakes at Pontefract in September. Shaped less well next time before again catching the eye dropped back in trip for a 6f novice stakes at Redcar in October, behind until staying on up the far side to finish never nearer fifth.

Not entirely 'thrown in' from an opening mark of 67 but not devoid of ability and confidently expected to flourish when stepped up in trip.

SHAREEF STAR (4YR BAY COLT)

TRAINER:	Sir Michael Stoute
PEDIGREE:	Sea The Stars – Gotlandia (Anabaa)
OPTIMUM TRIP:	1m 2f +
FORM:	042 – 0
RATING:	81

Sir Michael Stoute – keeping good company

First foal of Listed-winning half-sister to useful Gaiete from the family of Fillies' Mile winner Glorosia.

Has always been well regarded but not proved easy to train, unraced at two and retired for the season last June.

Very green on his debut when finishing behind in a 1m 3f maiden at Newbury last April. One-paced fourth of 16 next time in a 1m 2f Class 4 maiden at Newbury in May before running second, battling hard, to useful Piece Of History in a 1m maiden at Leicester in June.

Ran from a mark of 81 on his seasonal return in a 1m 2f 0-85 handicap at Doncaster but never saw daylight at any stage and failed to get in a challenge.

Far better than that and one to note when he is stepped up to a mile and a half, perhaps with one of the season's top middle-distance handicaps in mind.

Should progress beyond handicaps to greater heights.

SOVEREIGN GRANT (3YR BAY COLT)

TRAINER:	Sir Michael Stoute
PEDIGREE:	Kingman – Momentary (Nayef)
OPTIMUM TRIP:	1m +
FORM:	431 –
RATING:	86

Second foal and a half-brother to useful three-race winner Merlin out of a 1m 2f Listed winning half-sister to a winner. The second dam Fleeting Memory was a useful winning half-sister to a winner over hurdles.

Progressive form last season, shaping well in fourth on his debut in a 7f maiden at Sandown, short of room but plugging on up the hill, before possibly finding the quick ground against him when third of 11 at Yarmouth. Looked far more at home next time in a 7f novice stakes at Kempton, up there throughout and showing a bright turn of foot to beat Current Option very easily by three and a half lengths.

Was definitely going the right way last season and starts the new campaign on a workable mark. May stay beyond a mile and appeals as the right type for a valuable midsummer handicap.

SPARKLE IN HIS EYE (3YR CHESTNUT COLT)

TRAINER:	William Haggas
PEDIGREE:	Sea The Stars – Nyarhini (Fantastic Light)
OPTIMUM TRIP:	1m 4f
FORM:	21 –

Seventh foal and closely related to 7f/1m winner Token Of Love and a half-brother to four winners up to 1m 4f. Dam, a winner at 6f and 1m in the States, is a half-sister to the top-class Rebecca Sharp and to the dam of Golden Horn.

Superbly bred and confirmed the promise shown on his debut, when a very tenderly handled runner-up at Newcastle to the useful Set Piece, when coming from off the pace to get up close home and beat You Little Ripper in an extended 1m Class 5 back at Newcastle in January.

Has been carefully handled in both his races and bred to thrive when he is stepped up to middle distances. More than likely to prove up to Pattern class standard.

TABDEED (4YR CHESTNUT COLT)

TRAINER:	Owen Burrows
PEDIGREE:	Havana Gold – Puzzled (Peintre Celebre)
OPTIMUM TRIP:	6f
FORM:	1/101 –
RATING:	103

Second foal of a middle-distance placed daughter of Peintre Celebre from the family of Derby runner-up Walk In The Park and Irish 1,000 Guineas winner Classic Park.

A horse of great talent, quickening on the bridle to win his only start at two, and then successful on his seasonal return last May to win a 6f novice stakes at Nottingham going away with loads in hand.

Found things coming too soon for him when in mid-division stepped up to 7f in the Jersey Stakes at Royal Ascot before dropping to handicap company on his final start in a 6f 0-105 contest at Ascot, pulling hard and short of room before finding a scintillating turn of foot to put the race to bed inside the final furlong.

Has the potential to become a Group-class sprinter and warrants another try at that level. Travels very well through a race and has a potent turn of foot. Very useful.

Tabdeed – ready to take the next step up

THE DARK HORSES

The following horses, most of them unraced or lightly raced, have shaped with sufficient promise at home or on the track to warrant respect when they appear.

AL BATTAR (3YR BAY COLT)

TRAINER:	Ed Vaughan
PEDIGREE:	Dubawi – Giofra (Dansili)
OPTIMUM TRIP:	1m 4f
FORM:	0 –

Expensive, having cost €1,550,000 as a yearling, and second foal of Group 1 Falmouth Stakes winner and Hong Kong Cup runner-up Giofra, a winner of four races and a half-sister to seven winners including Listed winners Big Baz, Gradara and Gomati.

Shaped with great promise in a 1m Class 5 novice event at Kempton in December, well away before being shuffled back after a furlong, thereafter racing keenly until showing a useful turn of foot to make strong headway from the two-furlong pole to finish sixth, full of running, beaten two and a half lengths.

Bred to thrive over middle distances and has the potential to prove up to Pattern class. Very promising.

AZWAH (3YR BAY FILLY)

TRAINER:	Dermot Weld
PEDIGREE:	Invincible Spirit – Bethrah (Marju)
OPTIMUM TRIP:	1m
FORM:	Unraced

Fifth foal and closely related to a US 1m winner out of Irish 1,000 Guineas winner from the family of Group winner Reve D'Oscar and Numide.

Shows pace in her work at home and expected to prove at her most effective at trips up to a mile. Bred for fast ground.

CHABLIS (3YR BAY FILLY)

TRAINER:	Aidan O'Brien
PEDIGREE:	Galileo – Vadawina (Unfuwain)
OPTIMUM TRIP:	1m 4f
FORM:	1 –

Expensive 1,550,000gns yearling and ninth foal, a full sister to The Pentagon and a half-sister to five other winners including Vadamar and Vedouma.

Has a pedigree chock full of stamina, so did very well to win a fast-run 7f maiden at Gowran Park in October, well away and shuffled along in the straight to beat Peruvian Lily – now rated on 83 – by three-quarters of a length.

Bred to thrive over a mile and a half and one to have on the shortlist for an Oaks.

DAME MALLIOT (3YR BAY FILLY)

TRAINER:	Ed Vaughan
PEDIGREE:	Champs Elysees – Stars In Your Eyes (Galileo)
OPTIMUM TRIP:	1m 4f +
FORM:	1 –

Third living foal and a half-sister to useful sort Banksea and 1m 6f winner Stone The Crows out of a middle-distance winning three-parts sister to a Group-placed performer.

Shuffled along throughout when winning an extended 1m 1f auction novice stakes at Wolverhampton in December, staying on dourly from the home turn to beat an 80-rated rival into second.

Found this trip her absolute minimum and bred to thrive for middle distances and beyond. All about stamina.

EBBRAAM (3YR BAY FILLY)

TRAINER:	Simon Crisford
PEDIGREE:	Teofilo – Oojooba (Monsun)
OPTIMUM TRIP:	1m 2f +
FORM:	3 –

Second foal half-sister to a 1m-winning Listed-placed sister to dual-purpose performer High Bridge out of 1,000 Guineas winner Ameerat.

Slowly away and behind early stages, taken off her feet throughout, before finishing with a flourish in the final furlong to come home third to well-regarded Oaks entry Baba Ghanouj.

Takes after her dam's family and sure to progress over middle distances.

ELIGIBLE (3YR BAY GELDING)

TRAINER:	Clive Cox
PEDIGREE:	Dark Angel – Secrets Away (Refuse To Bend)
OPTIMUM TRIP:	7f
FORM:	00 –

130,000gns yearling second foal of a half-sister to US Grade 1 winner Hibaayeb out of a winning half-sister to smart 6f and 1m winner Zoning.

Showed little in two starts last season in 7f Class 4 contests at Newbury and Newmarket, displaying early pace on the first occasion and never figuring on the second.

Has some ability at home and may be one to consider for handicaps when he gets a mark.

FASHION'S STAR (3YR CHESTNUT FILLY)

TRAINER:	Roger Charlton
PEDIGREE:	Sea The Stars – Ninas Terz (Tertullian)
OPTIMUM TRIP:	1m 2f +
FORM:	1 –

Price rose from €100,000 as a yearling to €400,000 at two. Dam German Listed-placed two-year-old winner and a half-sister to Hong Kong middle-distance Group 1 winner Pakistan Star out of a German 1m 2f Listed winner from the family of German Oaks winner Next Gina.

Impressed when making her debut in a 7f Class 2 conditions stakes at Newbury in September, held up just off the pace and considerably handled to challenge and lead inside the final furlong, beating 86-rated Roxy Art with subsequent winner Ice Gala back in fourth.

Did well to win given the strong headwind, especially over a trip short of her requirements. Handled the ease in the ground but trainer thinks she will act on quicker going. Likely to earn black type at some point and entitled to improve for a step up in trip.

FAYLAQ (3YR BAY COLT)

TRAINER:	William Haggas
PEDIGREE:	Dubawi – Danedream (Lomitas)
OPTIMUM TRIP:	1m 4f
FORM:	00 –

Cost 1,500,000gns as a yearling and third foal of five-times Group 1 winner, including the Prix de l'Arc de Triomphe and King George, Danedream, herself a half-sister to four winners including 1m 4f Group 3 winner Venice Beach, from the family of French Leger winner Lady Berry. Second dam is a half-sister to seven winners.

Shaped with a modicum of promise in two starts in October last season, both 1m novice stakes at Newmarket, on his debut showing pace until weakening inside the final furlong and then next time coming with a steady challenge on the far side before fading close home.

Looked short of toe on both occasions and rolled around in the closing stages, perhaps not handling the track. Well regarded and bred to thrive over middle distances. Appeals as the sort to make his way up through the handicap ranks when he qualifies for a mark.

FIRST IN LINE (3YR CHESTNUT COLT)

TRAINER:	John Gosden
PEDIGREE:	New Approach – Hidden Hope (Daylami)
OPTIMUM TRIP:	1m 2f +
FORM:	Unraced

Seventh foal and full brother to 1m 4f winner Dawn Horizons and a half-brother to three winners including Listed winner Our Obsession out of a half-sister to Group 1 Coronation Stakes winner Rebecca Sharp from the family of Golden Horn.

Has shaped well at home and bred to suit middle distances. Likely to progress through the season.

FRANZ KAFKA (3YR CHESTNUT COLT)

TRAINER:	John Gosden
PEDIGREE:	Dubawi – Kailani (Monsun)
OPTIMUM TRIP:	1m 4f
FORM:	30 – 2
RATING:	82

Third foal and a full brother to 7f winner Kazimiera out of a 1m 2f Listed winning half-sister to UAE 1m 4f Group 1 winner Eastern Anthem and out of 1,000 Guineas and Oaks winner Kazzia.

Shaped very nicely on his debut in a 1m Class 4 novice stakes at Newmarket in October, looking one paced before staying on strongly in the closing stages to take third close home.

Odds-on to win a 1m Class 4 novice stakes next time at Newbury, took up the running two furlongs from home but failed to quicken and dropped back to sixth, beaten three lengths at the line.

Performed much better on his first run of this season over 7f at Doncaster chasing home previous winner 90-rated Fox Champion.

Bred to stay at least 1m 4f and now rated 82, he looks an ideal type for middle-distance and staying handicaps before progressing to greater heights.

GRENADIER GUARD (3YR CHESTNUT COLT)

TRAINER:	Mark Johnston
PEDIGREE:	Australia – Another Storm (Gone West)
OPTIMUM TRIP:	1m +
FORM:	Unraced

Eleventh foal and three-parts brother to Irish St Leger and Ascot Gold Cup winner Order Of St George and a half-brother to six winners including Group 3 winner Asperity.

Comes from a very successful family with a reputation for toughness so likely to thrive in the care of this particular trainer.

HUMANITARIAN (3YR BAY COLT)

TRAINER:	John Gosden
PEDIGREE:	Noble Mission – Sharbat (Dynaformer)
OPTIMUM TRIP:	1m 2f +
FORM:	21 –

Sixth foal and half-brother to three winners at up to a mile out of a US winning half-sister to middle-distance Group 3 winner Pomology.

Shaped very well when staying on into second behind Kick On in a 1m maiden at Newmarket that turned out well before quickening from a handy position to beat subsequent winner Sash, now rated 82, by five lengths in a 1m novice stakes at Lingfield in November.

Ran to a mark in the high 80s at Lingfield and may improve beyond handicaps. Appears to possess a turn of foot.

IMPERIAL CHARM (3YR BAY FILLY)

TRAINER:	Simon Crisford
PEDIGREE:	Dubawi – Reem Three (Mark Of Esteem)
OPTIMUM TRIP:	1m 4f +
FORM:	331 – 2
RATING:	86

Seventh foal and a half-sister to Group 1 Prix Jean Romanet winner Ajman Princess, useful performer Naqshabban up to 1m 4f, Group 2 1m winner Ostilio and 7f winner Cape Byron.

Simon Crisford – should have more reasons to celebrate

The dam, a winner of three races, was Listed placed and is a half-sister to three winners including Group 2 Celebration Mile winner Afsare. Second dam Jumaireyah is a half-sister to numerous winners including useful stayer Lost Soldier Three and middle-distance winner Altaweelah.

Shaped very well when third, keeping on at one pace, to Layaleena and Ice Gala in 7f fillies' novice stakes at Newmarket in August. Looked uncomfortable on the good to firm ground when third next time to Sunday Star in a 7f maiden at Newmarket before staying on strongly on soft ground to win a 7f novice stakes at Newmarket in November.

Now rated 86, she improved when stepped up to a mile in a Group 3 at Longchamp in April, finishing second to previous winner Castle Lady. Could improve further over 1m 2f or more.

INVICTUS SPIRIT (3YR BAY COLT)

TRAINER:	Sir Michael Stoute
PEDIGREE:	Frankel – Daring Aim (Daylami)
OPTIMUM TRIP:	1m 2f +
FORM:	Unraced

Ninth foal and a three-parts brother to useful Bold Sniper and a half-brother to five winners, including Listed winner Daphne and Highland Glen, out of a middle-distance winning half-sister to Oaks runner-up Flight Of Fancy.

Had shown ability in his work until sustaining an injury. Should recover and expected to develop into a useful middle-distance performer.

JUBILOSO (3YR BAY FILLY)

TRAINER:	Sir Michael Stoute
PEDIGREE:	Shamardal – Joyeuse (Oasis Dream)
OPTIMUM TRIP:	7f +
FORM:	Unraced

First foal of a 6f Listed winning full sister to Morpheus and a half-sister to unbeaten champion Frankel and middle-distance Group 1 winner Noble Mission.

Comes from a brilliant family and only has to win to ensure her future for the paddocks. Shaped well in her work at home last season and has the pedigree to go places.

KISS FOR A JEWEL (3YR BAY FILLY)

TRAINER:	Dermot Weld
PEDIGREE:	Kingman – Sapphire (Medicean)
OPTIMUM TRIP:	1m +
FORM:	2 –

Second foal of a Group 2 1m 4f British Champions Fillies' and Mares Stakes winner plus two Group 3 races, a half-sister to Group 1 Prince Of Wales's Stakes winner Free Eagle and useful triple Group 2 and triple Group 3 winner Custom Cut.

Second dam Polished Gem is a full sister to US Grade 1 winner and Group 2 Sun Chariot Stakes winner Dress To Thrill and a half-sister to seven winners.

Would possibly have made a winning debut in an extended 1m maiden at Galway in October but for running green, outpaced in the early stages and then not handling the home turn. Looked likely to prevail a furlong from home before being edged out by the more experienced winner, now rated on 91, and finishing five and a half lengths clear of the third.

Rated one of the yard's better fillies and will probably earn black type somewhere along the line.

LOCH LAGGAN (3YR BAY COLT)

TRAINER:	David Menuisier
PEDIGREE:	Sea The Stars – Magic Sister (Cadeaux Genereux)
OPTIMUM TRIP:	1m 2f +
FORM:	O

Ninth foal and full brother to 1m 2f winner Karawaan and half-brother to Group 1 winner Rajeem and 1m 1f winner Flannery. Dam is a full sister to Prix Morny and Molecomb Stakes winner Hoh Magic.

Disappointed when beating only one home on his debut in a 12-runner Newbury maiden over 1m in April, but has shown ability at home and ought to improve in time when stepped up in trip.

LOGICIAN (3YR ROAN COLT)

TRAINER:	John Gosden
PEDIGREE:	Frankel – Scuffle (Daylami)
OPTIMUM TRIP:	1m 2f +
FORM:	Unraced

Fifth foal and a full brother to 1m 2f winner Collide and a half-brother to three winners including US Grade 3 winner Suffused. Dam a winning half-sister to Group 1 winner Cityscape.

Shaped well last season and bred to appreciate a mile and a quarter or more.

Ed Vaughan – quietly making a name for himself

MAGIC J (3YR CHESTNUT COLT)

TRAINER:	Ed Vaughan
PEDIGREE:	Scat Daddy – Miss Lamour (Mr Greeley)
OPTIMUM TRIP:	7f +
FORM:	1 –

$950,000 yearling first foal of US dirt winning half-sister to Graded stakes-placed 1m winner Tejida out of US Grade 3 winning half-sister to the dam of Eclipse Stakes winner Hawkbill from a good US family.

Formerly named Ginger Wolverine before his debut, was very well backed to make a winning debut in a 6f Class 4 novice stakes at Yarmouth in September, travelling well before responding to hand riding to beat Swindler and Excelled, each now on 82, with next-time winner Mubakker in fourth.

Had shown plenty of ability in his work at home and ran to a mark in the mid-80s at Yarmouth. Bred to suit quick ground and may be the right type for the Jersey Stakes.

MANNGUY (3YR BAY COLT)

TRAINER:	Simon Crisford
PEDIGREE:	Oasis Dream – Galaxy Highflyer (Galileo)
OPTIMUM TRIP:	1m +
FORM:	Unraced

Seventh foal and a full brother to Group-placed Oklahoma City out of an unraced daughter of Galileo from the family of top stayer and now sire Kayf Tara and Group 1 middle-distance performer Opera House, from the family of Colorspin.

Impeccably bred and expected to stay beyond a mile despite the speed influence of his sire.

MAWSOOF (3YR BAY COLT)

TRAINER:	Saeed bin Suroor
PEDIGREE:	Distorted Humor – Tafaneen (Dynaformer)
OPTIMUM TRIP:	1m 2f +
FORM:	Unraced

Third foal and half-brother to 1m 2f winner Tamleek and 1m winner Watheeqa out of a daughter of Dynaformer from the family of US Grade 1 winner Riskaverse.

Has shown ability in his work at home and expected to take quite high rank this summer.

MIA MARIA (3YR GREY FILLY)

TRAINER:	Dermot Weld
PEDIGREE:	Dansili – Majestic Silver (Linamix)
OPTIMUM TRIP:	1m 4f +
FORM:	3 –

Fifth foal full sister to dual Group 3 and dual Listed winner Carla Bianca and a half-sister to 7f winner and Group 2 Beresford Stakes runner-up True Solitaire, German Listed winner Joailliere and useful 7f and 1m performer Cascavelle.

The dam is an unraced half-sister to useful Group 3 stayer Profound Beauty and fair 1m 2f winner Rock Critic. Second dam Diamond Trim is a Listed winner of five races and a half-sister to five winners including Ribblesdale Stakes winner Irresistible Jewel.

Bred to stay well and that is how it looked on her debut in a 1m maiden at Gowran Park in September, up there just off the pace before running very green and wandering in the straight. Plugged on to finish a one-paced third beaten nine lengths by the winner.

Looks sure to appreciate a distance of ground.

NAME THE WIND (3YR BAY COLT)

TRAINER:	James Tate
PEDIGREE:	Toronado – Trust The Wind (Dansili)
OPTIMUM TRIP:	1m 2f +
FORM:	1 –

Second foal of winning three-parts sister to 1m Group 3 winner Hathal and a half-sister to 1m 2f Group 3 winner Gentleman's Deal.

Narrow but cosy winner of a 7f novice stakes at Kempton in September, up with the pace and just getting the better of 2/9 chance Buffalo River, a winner next time and now rated on 89. Did well to win over the trip given the stamina on his distaff side.

Ran to a mark in the low 90s but should be better than that when stepped up in trip, possibly capable of earning black type at some stage.

NANTUCKET (3YR BAY FILLY)

TRAINER:	Sir Michael Stoute
PEDIGREE:	Sea The Stars – Lucy Cavendish (Elusive Quality)
OPTIMUM TRIP:	1m +
FORM:	0–

Half-sister to 1m 2f and 1m 4f winner Light Of Asia, six-race Italian winner Caveran and 7f winner In Her Stride. Dam an unraced half-sister to seven winners including the Group 3 1m Prix des Reservoirs winner and Group 1 third Summertime Legacy, dam of Group 1 winners Wavering and Mandaean. Family traces back to Derby winner Golden Fleece.

Made her sole appearance in a 7f Class 5 novice stakes at Kempton in November, racing in mid-division throughout and keeping on steadily towards the finish, never nearer.

Apparently quite well regarded by her trainer and can win a maiden at least before seeking black type.

PASEO (3YR BAY GELDING)

TRAINER:	Amanda Perrett
PEDIGREE:	Champs Elysees – Posteritas (Lear Fan)
OPTIMUM TRIP:	1m 2f +
FORM:	Unraced

Brother to French 1m winner Starflower and half-brother to Group 1 Prix Jean Prat winner Mutual Trust, triple 1m winner Kryptos, the stayer Pilansberg and other winners.

The dam, a listed 1m 2f winner, is a half-sister to five winners including Apex Star and the second dam Imroz won and was Listed placed and is a half-sister to five winners.

Described as a lovely horse, he has displayed some talent and may show up well in an early maiden.

PEARL OF MANAMA (3YR BAY FILLY)

TRAINER:	Martyn Meade
PEDIGREE:	Scat Daddy – Auction (Mr Greeley)
OPTIMUM TRIP:	1m
FORM:	Unraced

Cost $800,000 as a yearling and the first foal of a winning and Listed-placed half-sister to a Japanese Group 3 winner from a middle-distance Italian family.

Has shown pace in her work at home.

Camelot – proving himself as a sire

QUEEN GUANHUMARA (3YR BAY FILLY)

TRAINER:	Henry De Bromhead
PEDIGREE:	Camelot – Ambitious Lady (Anabaa)
OPTIMUM TRIP:	1m 2f +
FORM:	0 – 0

Eighth foal and half-sister to three winners including All Best Friends, a sprint winner in Australia and Hong Kong, and Career, a winner over 7f in Australia. Dam unraced half-sister to 1m Group 3 winner Anna Palariva, the dam of Irish 1,000 Guineas second Anna Salai, out of Park Hill Stakes winner Anna Of Saxony.

Shaped quite well when ninth of 12 in a 7f maiden at Naas in September. Showed rather more on her seasonal return in a 1m 2f fillies maiden at Leopardstown, behind early stages and then progress around the home turn, running wide but staying on steadily all the way to the line to finish a never-nearer sixth.

Has the pedigree and ability to win over a mile and a half, probably at a reasonably high level.

RAINBOW HEART (3YR BAY FILLY)

TRAINER:	William Haggas
PEDIGREE:	Born To Sea – Sea Of Heartbreak (Rock Of Gibraltar)
OPTIMUM TRIP:	1m 2f +
FORM:	31 –

Second foal out of middle-distance Group 2-winning half-sister to German 1m 3f Listed winner Persefona from the family of Irish 1,000 Guineas and Yorkshire Oaks winner Sarah Siddons.

Made an eye-catching debut to finish third in a 7f maiden at Newmarket in September, powering through from arrears until tiring in the final furlong. Confirmed that favourable impression in no uncertain terms just under a month later in a 7f novice auction contest, making all to beat subsequent winner Pytilia by eight lengths.

Runner-up now rated on 77, so winner ran to a mark in the low 90s. Performance warrants taking her chance in an Oaks trial and has the pedigree to stay the trip. Hard to assess at this stage but probably Group class.

SET PIECE (3YR BAY COLT)

TRAINER:	Hugo Palmer
PEDIGREE:	Dansili – Portodora (Kingmambo)
OPTIMUM TRIP:	1m 2f +
FORM:	11 –
RATING:	86

Sixth foal and full brother to 7f winner Tempera and half-brother to three winners at up to 1m 2f. Dam won over 7f from the family of top-class performer Reams Of Verse.

Displayed an impressive turn of foot when making a winning debut in a 1m Class 5 novice event at Kempton in December, well away before losing his place when clipping heels after two furlongs. Still only sixth inside the final furlong before bursting through between horses to win going away by a length from Just The Man and subsequent dual winner Creationist.

Followed that up in January in a 1m Class 4 novice stakes at Newcastle, slowly away from the stalls but travelling smoothly throughout and moving ahead comfortably to hold the challenge of the tenderly handled subsequent winner Sparkle In His Eye.

Definitely has the potential to prove superior to his mark, probably at Listed or Group level. Bred to relish a step up to 1m 2f or more and appears to possess a turn of foot. Exciting.

SILENT HUNTER (3YR BAY COLT)

TRAINER:	Saeed bin Suroor
PEDIGREE:	Dutch Art – Yellow Rosebud (Jeremy)
OPTIMUM TRIP:	1m 2f +
FORM:	42 –

Second foal of a dual Group 3-winning half-sister to five winners including Listed winner and Group 3 placed Seeharn. Second dam Nebraas is an unraced half-sister to six winners including Group 1 Golden Jubilee Stakes winner Malhub.

Shaped well in his two starts last season, putting in good late work to finish fourth in a 7f novice stakes on his debut and then showing a bright turn of foot in defeat when second to Nivaldo in a 1m novice stakes at Kempton in November. Third and fourth subsequent winners.

Not given a hard time last season and appeals as the type to progress from a maiden through to a valuable midsummer handicap. Appears to have a turn of foot.

SURFMAN (3YR BAY COLT)

TRAINER:	Roger Varian
PEDIGREE:	Kingman – Shimmering Surf (Danehill Dancer)
OPTIMUM TRIP:	1m +
FORM:	31 –

Third foal and a half-brother to middle-distance Group 1 winner Kitesurf out of Group 3 winning daughter of useful Sun On The Sea.

Slowly away and very green throughout when staying on strongly into third in an extended 1m maiden at Nottingham in October.

Kingman - on the cusp of becoming a top-class sire

Returned there just under a month later to beat Durston by one and three-quarter lengths, handling the softer ground well.

Hard to assess on the evidence to hand but looked very progressive from his first to second run and is well regarded by his trainer. Probably capable of working up to Pattern-class company through handicaps.

SWIFT WING (3YR CHESTNUT COLT)

TRAINER:	John Gosden
PEDIGREE:	Pivotal - Gull Wing (In The Wings)
OPTIMUM TRIP:	1m 2f +
FORM:	Unraced

Seventh foal and a full brother to middle-distance Group 2 King Edward VII Stakes winner and King George VI and Queen Elizabeth Stakes runner-up Eagle Top, 1m 2f Group 2 Dante Stakes winner

Wings Of Desire and 1m 6f Group 2 winner The Lark. Dam a tough 1m 6f Listed winner and a half-sister to Oaks winner Sariska.

A product of one of the most successful families in racing and has apparently shown he has inherited some of that talent in work at home.

WINGS OF TIME (3YR BAY GELDING)

TRAINER:	Charlie Appleby
PEDIGREE:	Invincible Spirit – Marie De Medici (Medicean)
OPTIMUM TRIP:	1m +
FORM:	0 – 1

Fifth foal and a full brother to Local Time, a winner at around a mile, and a half-brother to 1m 2f winner Extra Mile and 1m 3f winner Beauvais. Dam, a Listed winner at 1m 2f, is a half-sister to Group 1 middle-distance winner Erupt.

Hopelessly green on his debut in a 7f Class 4 maiden contest at Newmarket in September, slowly away and hanging in arrears, until making late headway when the race was over.

Knew more about the job next time in an extended 1m Class 5 maiden at Wolverhampton, heavily supported to odds-on and settled just off the pace before powering through on the rails to win cosily by half a length from Reggae Runner, a winner next time and now rated on 82, and third home Solar Heights, a winner at Chelmsford and now rated on 76.

Ran to a mark in the mid-80s through this form, but is potentially superior to that. Could be very interesting in a handicap.

THE DARK HANDICAPPERS

The following horses left the impression that they were being trained last season with handicaps in mind.

AUTONOMY (3YR BAY GELDING)

TRAINER:	Sir Mark Prescott
PEDIGREE:	Dansili – Funsie (Saumarez)
OPTIMUM TRIP:	1m 4f +
FORM:	000 –
RATING:	58

Tenth foal and a half-brother to four winners including Derby winner Authorized and 1m 4f winner Empowered. Dam an unraced half-sister to a Group 3 winner.

Improved with each outing, staying on steadily into seventh in a 7f novice stakes at Wolverhampton and then again making a little late headway over an extended mile there in October.

Mark of 58 seems fair taking lines through the winner and second in his final start, especially given the strong likelihood of improvement when stepped up in trip.

BABBO'S BOY (3YR GREY COLT)

TRAINER:	Michael Bell
PEDIGREE:	Mastercraftsman – Bunood (Sadler's Wells)
OPTIMUM TRIP:	1m 4f
FORM:	O4 –

Eighth foal and half-brother to three winners at up to a mile out of a daughter of Sadler's Wells that was Group-placed at 1m 6f from the family of Cheveley Park Stakes winner Desirable.

Stepped up markedly on his first run when staying on steadily to finish fourth to Good Birthday in a 1m novice stakes at Newbury in October, never nearer than at the finish.

Form reads quite well, with winner successful again since and now rated on 90. Requires one more run for a handicap mark and has the potential to develop into a useful staying handicapper.

CRANEUR (3YR CHESTNUT GELDING)

TRAINER:	Harry Dunlop
PEDIGREE:	Showcasing – Paris Winds (Galileo)
OPTIMUM TRIP:	1m +
FORM:	OOO –
RATING:	66

Fifth living foal of well-related 1m-winning daughter of Galileo, related to winners up to a mile.

Has run with great promise on all three starts, plugging on when green to finish a never-nearer eighth of 14 to Stormwave in a 1m novice stakes at Salisbury in October. Shaped even better when fourth of 11 to Art Song in a 1m novice stakes at Kempton, before shaping very well when seventh of 13 to highly promising Zakouski

Harry Dunlop – with friends

and Headman in a 7f novice stakes at Kempton.

Looks extremely favourably handicapped given the company he has kept and has to win races from this mark. Could look very well bought at 12,500gns as a yearling. Very interesting indeed.

DALAALAAT (3YR BAY COLT)

TRAINER:	William Haggas
PEDIGREE:	Kingman – Gile Na Greine (Galileo)
OPTIMUM TRIP:	1m 2f
FORM:	01 –

Fourth foal and closely related to 6f winner Ghanimah and half-brother to 1m winner Alwahsh and 1m 1f winner Mawjood, all three trained in this yard. Dam 7f winner and 1,000 Guineas third, a sister to Group 3 winners Cuis Ghaire and Scintillula.

Showed up well on his debut in a 1m novice stakes at Sandown in September and built on that next time in an extended 1m maiden at Nottingham, beating subsequent winner King Of Change cosily with more in hand than the half-length margin suggests.

Fourth now rated 71 so mark for this horse likely to be in the mid to high 70s.

EARL OF HARROW (3YR BAY GELDING)

TRAINER:	Mick Channon
PEDIGREE:	Sixties Icon – The Screamer (Insan)
OPTIMUM TRIP:	1m 2f +
FORM:	000 –
RATING:	67

Tenth foal and a full brother to useful performer Juventas and a half-brother to middle-distance and hurdle winners up to 2m 5f.

Revealed a hint of ability in three starts last season, over 1m 2f and then twice over 1m 1f, plugging on steadily on the third occasion in a 1m 1f novice stakes at Redcar.

Hardly 'thrown in' from his opening mark but likely to win races when stepped up to middle distances and beyond. Probably prefers soft ground.

GREAT BEAR (3YR BAY COLT)

TRAINER:	Roger Charlton
PEDIGREE:	Dansili – Great Heavens (Galileo)
OPTIMUM TRIP:	1m 4f
FORM:	1 –

Third foal half-brother to 1m winner Dubhe out of Group 1 Irish Oaks and Group 2 Lancashire Oaks winner Great Heavens, a full sister to the top-class Nathaniel and a half-sister to eight winners including Group 1 Fillies' Mile winner Playful Act, Group 3 winner Percussionist and Group 2 Sun Chariot Stakes winner Echoes In Eternity.

Made his debut in an extended 1m Class 5 novice stakes at Wolverhampton in November, tracking leader off a moderate pace and green on home turn, hanging left, before buckling down tenaciously as stamina kicked in to hold the strong-finishing Copal, now rated 78, by half a length.

Ran to a mark of about 80 at Wolverhampton and could prove very effective off that rating over a distance of ground.

HIGHLAND SKY (4YR BAY GELDING)

TRAINER:	David Simcock
PEDIGREE:	Camelot – Healing Music (Bering)
OPTIMUM TRIP:	2m
FORM:	00/0300134 –
RATING:	68

Three-parts brother to middle-distance and hurdle winner Kuda Huraa and a half-brother to three winners including Derby runner-up At First Sight.

A little bit of an underachiever but seems significant that he has been kept in training and capable of winning more races from this mark. Shaped well in third off 67 on his handicap debut at Redcar in May before rising in grade to finish a good fifth to Ghostwatch in a 1m 6f Class 4 at Sandown.

Never going next time at Chelmsford before winning a 1m 6f 0-70 at Lingfield, well backed beforehand and responding to firm driving to win by one and a quarter lengths. Unsuited by the steady pace and rain-softened ground next time at Goodwood before running well below form in a 2m 0-80 at Kempton.

Not an obvious inclusion in this section but appeals as the type to win a few more races on quick ground over two miles.

LADY BOWTHORPE (3YR BAY FILLY)

TRAINER:	William Jarvis
PEDIGREE:	Nathaniel – Maglietta Fina (Verglas)
OPTIMUM TRIP:	1m 4f +
FORM:	4 –

Second foal and a half-sister to 6f Listed and Group 3 winner Speak In Colours out of a 5f and 7f five-race winning half-sister to four winners including 1m and 1m 2f Group 2 winner Tullius.

Second dam Whipped Queen won twice and is a half-sister to nine winners including Group 1 placed Monsagem and US Grade 3 winner Pie In Your Eye. Pedigree enhanced by last season's exploits of Speak In Colours.

Shaped quite well given the 6f trip on her debut in a Class 4 novice stakes at Yarmouth in September, travelling well on the far side of the field and every chance until tiring in the final furlong.

Showed good pace given her stout pedigree and looks one to bear in mind for 1m 2f or more handicaps, hopefully off a favourable mark following two more runs.

MILLERS CREEK (3YR BAY GELDING)

TRAINER:	Sir Mark Prescott
PEDIGREE:	Aussie Rules – Miss Katmandu (Rainbow Quest)
OPTIMUM TRIP:	1m 2f +
FORM:	000 –
RATING:	53

Eighth foal and full brother to Tenzing Norgay, a winner up to 1m 5f, and a half-brother to 2m winner Kashgar and 1m 2f winner Miss

Turpan. Dam once-raced half-sister to Ormonde Stakes winner St Expedit and Asian Heights.

Did not shape with obvious promise in three starts, twice over seven furlongs and once over a mile, but likely to show more over middle distances.

OUR OYSTERCATCHER (5YR BROWN GELDING)

TRAINER:	Mark Pattinson
PEDIGREE:	Pastoral Pursuits – The Dark Eider (Superlative)
OPTIMUM TRIP:	5f
FORM:	10/30210 –
RATING:	75

From the family of Ormonde Stakes winner The Whistling Teal but this one all speed as he showed when making all from a high draw to beat 16 rivals in a Class 5 0-70 at Bath in October.

Missed the break next time out at Nottingham but can win again from his current mark. One to catch fresh.

ROAD TO PARIS (3YR BAY GELDING)

TRAINER:	Sir Mark Prescott
PEDIGREE:	Champs Elysees – Alchemilla (Dubai Destination)
OPTIMUM TRIP:	1m 4f +
FORM:	000 –
RATING:	60

Fifth foal three-parts brother to 1m Listed winner Smugglers Moon, later a dual winner when renamed Gold Land in Hong Kong, and half-brother to Stardrifter, a winner up to 1m 1f. Dam unraced half-sister to Group 2 winner Strategic Prince from the family of top stayer Yorkshire I and Oaks, Irish Oaks and Yorkshire Oaks winner Ramruma.

Showed a hint of ability in three runs last season, all over seven furlongs, twice at Kempton and once at Lingfield. Shaped best on final start at Lingfield, green and possibly unsuited to the track but still in touch early in straight before plugging on to finish a never-nearer sixth.

Fairly treated on 60, taking various lines, and entitled to improve for a step up to middle distances.

SOCRU (3YR BAY GELDING)

TRAINER:	Mick Easterby
PEDIGREE:	Kodiac – Hemaris (Sri Pekan)
OPTIMUM TRIP:	6f +
FORM:	00244 –
RATING:	67

Third foal of a 6f-winning half-sister to Group 3 winner Snaefell, 6f Listed winner Daganya and the tough sprint handicapper Henry Hall.

Shaped well in two starts for former handler Jamie Osborne and was claimed by this trainer for £18,000 after finishing a fair fifth of 18 in a valuable 6f seller at York in June. Ran well on his first start for new connections when second of eight to Gabrial The Wire in a 6f novice stakes at Chester.

Again performed with credit on his next two starts, fourth of nine in a 6f nursery at Pontefract in October and then fourth of 11 three weeks later in a 7f 0-70 nursery at Leicester, staying on down the far side of the group having stumbled approaching the two-furlong pole.

May be better at six furlongs than seven but in good hands to win a northern sprint handicap or two.

THANKS BE (3YR CHESTNUT FILLY)

TRAINER:	Charlie Fellowes
PEDIGREE:	Mukhadram – Out Of Thanks (Sadler's Wells)
OPTIMUM TRIP:	1m +
FORM:	00 –

Ninth foal and a half-sister to 6f Group 3 winner Love Lockdown, 7f and 1m winners Chosen Character and Spryt and 1m winner Cocktail Hour. Dam a winner over 1m 2f from the family of Irish 1,000 Guineas winner Trusted Partner.

Quite highly tried on her debut in a 7f Class 2 conditions stakes at Newbury, up there for a long way until weakening inside the final furlong, beaten four and a quarter lengths by Fashion's Star. Quietly backed next time out, down in trip for a 6f Class 5 maiden at Kempton, showed good speed for a long way until dropping out of contention inside the final furlong.

Shows plenty of pace given her relatively stout bottom line. Likely to come into her own once she is qualified for handicaps.

VENTURE (3YR BAY GELDING)

TRAINER:	Clive Cox
PEDIGREE:	Showcasing – Starfly (Invincible Spirit)
OPTIMUM TRIP:	6f
FORM:	04 –

Speedily bred €230,000 yearling purchase half-brother to 6f and 7f winner Harry Speed out of a 5f winning half-sister to French 6f Listed winner Mytographie out of a French winning half-sister to 1m Group 3 winner Malaspina.

Has shown sufficient ability to suggest races will come his way, notably when given a considerate ride to finish sixth of 13 to Dirty Rascal on his racecourse debut in a 6f Class 4 novice stakes at Windsor in September.

Again shaped well in a 6f Class 5 novice stakes at Kempton in October, switched inside from his wide draw and travelling just off the pace throughout, staying on without quickening to finish fourth.

Not bred to stay much beyond 6f but runs as if he could.

ZUBA (3YR BAY COLT)

TRAINER:	Amanda Perrett
PEDIGREE:	Dubawi – Purr Along (Mount Nelson)
OPTIMUM TRIP:	1m 2f +
FORM:	001 –
RATING:	75

First foal of winner of three races including two Group 3 contests and a half-sister to five winners including the speedy Katawi. Second dam Purring, a winner at 7f, is a half-sister to Falmouth Stakes and Prix de Sandringham winner Ronda.

Showed little on his debut in a 1m Class 4 maiden at Newmarket but shaped far better next time in a 1m 1f Class 4 novice stakes at Goodwood, racing handily in fourth until tiring in the straight before staying on steadily in the final furlong.

Not unfancied next time when stepped up in trip for a 1m 2f Class 5 maiden at Chelmsford, switching to challenge two furlongs out and responding well to beat Say The Word by a length.

Has always shown something at home but bred to stay well and will need 1m 4f or more to optimise his potential. Not badly treated on his opening mark of 75.

Marten's Telephone Information Line
Established 1980

If you want to keep in touch with Marten's latest thoughts ring him on:

0906 150 1555

Selections given in the first minute
(calls charged at £1.50 a minute at all times)
May cost more from a mobile

A non-premium rate version of this line is available for subscription. Please call the office if you'd like to join our Telephone & Text service.

Too Darn Hot – will he deliver?

THE QIPCO 2,000 GUINEAS PREVIEW

Horses listed in order of betting at time of writing.

TOO DARN HOT (JOHN GOSDEN)

Full brother to So Mi Dar, winner of a Group 3 over an extended 1m 2f, and Lah Ti Dar, winner of a 1m 4f Listed race and runner-up in the St Leger, out of triple Group 1 winner Dar Re Mi. Bred to stay 1m 4f but trainer has doubts, believing 1m 2f may be as far as he wants.

Unbeaten in four starts, on his debut at Sandown over a mile and then three times over 7f in Group 3 Solario Stakes, Group 2 Champagne Stakes and Group 1 Dewhurst Stakes. Has needed stoking up on every occasion before striding clear to win going away. On latest occasion in the Dewhurst momentarily looked in trouble before switching right to move upsides and pull clear from the winner of the Group 1 Phoenix Stakes.

Can be a little keen in the early stages and did not appear to have great scope at two. May be vulnerable to a late developer or a rival with more toe in the Guineas and likely to reach his peak when stepped up to 1m 2f or further. Appeals more as a Derby type despite trainer's qualms.

QUORTO (CHARLIE APPLEBY)

First foal by Dubawi out of 1m 2f winner and Oaks and Irish Oaks third Volume from the family of a 2m 4f Prix Cadran winner. Bred to stay beyond a mile, probably middle distances.

Did well given his pedigree to make a winning debut in a 6f novice stakes at Newmarket in June, quickening discernibly to win going away. Three weeks later scampered clear to beat Cape Of Good Hope, now rated 106, in the Group 2 Superlative Stakes over 7f before beating Anthony Van Dyck in the Group 1 National Stakes at the Curragh.

Prone to hang a little once clear and turn of foot possibly not as effective on the easy ground at the Curragh as it was on good to firm going in his previous two starts. Has almost three lengths to find with Too Darn Hot on a line through Anthony Van Dyck but may have the superior turn of foot.

Reported injured and will miss the Guineas but would warrant serious respect were he to return for the Derby. Showed great tenacity in Ireland and has gears.

TEN SOVEREIGNS (AIDAN O'BRIEN)

By the speedy No Nay Never out of the Exceed And Excel mare Seeking Solace, a winner over 1m 2f and runner-up in a Listed 1m 3f. Half-brother to a 1m winner in Spain.

Unbeaten in three starts, winning a 6f maiden at the Curragh in August and then a Group 3 at the Curragh, before beating Jash by half a length in the Group 1 Middle Park Stakes at Newmarket.

Ran on very gamely at Newmarket to repel the runner-up despite tending to carry his head a little high. Wasn't stopping at the end of his races despite his very strong speed-based pedigree.

Trainer has doubts about his staying a mile but will probably still be tried in the Guineas. Very classy and sure to win again at the highest level, possibly at sprint trips.

CALYX (JOHN GOSDEN)

Bred along miling lines, by Kingman out of 1m Group 3 winner Helleborine from the family of Distant Music.

Appeared to quicken when winning a 6f novice stakes on his debut at Newmarket in June. Stepped up considerably in grade 10 days later to beat 22 rivals in the Group 2 Coventry Stakes, taking up the running on the nearside two furlongs out and keeping on well to beat subsequent Group 2 and Group 1 winner Advertise, next time runner-up to Too Darn Hot in the Dewhurst Stakes.

Not as impressive in his races as the three above him in the betting but has done well since his setback. Trainer says he will be entered for the Commonwealth Cup over six furlongs. Looks tough and a line through Advertise casts him in a favourable light.

MAGNA GRECIA (AIDAN O'BRIEN)

Invincible Spirit fifth foal of a 7f Group 3-winning daughter of Galileo. Related to winners at up to 1m 2f.

Came through smoothly on the rails to make a winning debut in a 7f maiden at Naas in September. Found the very useful Persian King a neck too smart for him in the 1m Group 3 Godolphin Autumn Stakes at Newmarket before doing just enough to edge out Phoenix Of Spain in the Group 1 Vertem Futurity Trophy at Doncaster.

A line through Phoenix Of Spain puts him within 3lb of Too Darn Hot but still looked green at Doncaster and may have more in hand than appearances suggest. Already proven at a mile and should stay further.

ADVERTISE (MARTYN MEADE)

Has a profound speed bias to his pedigree, being by Showcasing out of a 6f-winning daughter of Pivotal.

Impressed when coming with a long run from off the pace to beat 11 rivals in a 6f maiden at Newbury in May. Again came through strongly at the finish when beaten a length by Calyx at Royal Ascot, racing away from the winner, before beating Konchek by two lengths in the 6f July Stakes at Newmarket. Had more use made of him when responding gamely to win the Group 1 Phoenix Stakes at the Curragh before proving unable to live with Too Darn Hot in the closing stages of the Dewhurst.

Stayed the 7f quite well at Newmarket but far from certain to get a mile, although he will probably be tried in the Guineas. A very tough competitive colt with more scope than most. Sure to prove competitive at the highest level but unproven on easy ground.

PERSIAN KING (ANDRE FABRE)

Kingman second foal of a 1m 2f-winning relative to Group 1 winner Planteur from a strong middle-distance family.

Won twice over a mile in France by wide margins, before beating subsequent Group 1 winner Magna Grecia with nothing in hand in the Group 3 Godolphin Autumn Stakes at Newmarket. Travelled very well through the early stages of the race and may have been ill at ease on the quicker ground and undulations in the closing stages.

Proven over a mile but reported unlikely to tackle the Guineas. Top class prospect but may be best suited to easy ground.

ANTHONY VAN DYCK (AIDAN O'BRIEN)

Galileo half-brother to winners up to a mile out of Australian sprint-winning daughter of Exceed And Excel.

Experienced, having raced seven times at two, displaying great tenacity both in victory and defeat. Won three on the bounce in July and August, notably a Group 3 and a Group 2, before finding Quorto one and a quarter lengths too smart for him in the Group 1 National Stakes at the Curragh. Again outpointed but not disgraced in the Dewhurst Stakes, up there but unable to keep tabs with Advertise and Too Darn Hot, beaten four lengths by the winner in third. Ninth of 14 on his final start at Churchill Downs.

Kept busy at two and probably a few pounds short of the best, but blessed with an admirable temperament and acts on both easy and fast ground. May be best at trips short of a mile.

JASH (SIMON CRISFORD)

Second foal by Kodiac out of 6f-winning daughter of Dutch Art, from the family of Group 1 and Grade winner Hibaayeb.

Quickened impressively once the penny dropped to win a 6f novice stakes at Newmarket in August before hacking up to land long odds-on in a 6f novice stakes at Salisbury. Shaped very well when stepped up to Group 1 Middle Park Stakes 15 days later, travelling well and running Ten Sovereigns to half a length and finishing over three lengths clear of the third.

Should stay a mile but perhaps not much further. Races with great enthusiasm and was progressing very well last season. Acts on fast ground and appeals as one of the better longshots for the Guineas. May start his season in the Greenham.

LINE OF DUTY (CHARLIE APPLEBY)

By Galileo and fourth foal of Jacqueline Quest, disqualified after winning the 1,000 Guineas, and a full brother to winners up to 1m 2f.

Had no luck on his debut when runner-up, beaten a fast-diminishing neck, at Sandown before running second at Haydock, racing alone, and then overcoming trouble yet again to win a 1m maiden at Goodwood. Beat Syrtis in a 1m 1f Group 3 at Chantilly before landing the Breeders' Cup Juvenile Turf at Churchill Downs in November.

Has something to find with the best but has a likeable attitude and looks sure to get 1m 2f and further.

MADHMOON (KEVIN PRENDERGAST)

By Dawn Approach out of a Group-placed daughter of Haafhd, effective at around 1m 2f.

Showed a turn of foot to beat Sydney Opera House in a 1m maiden at Leopardstown in August and then improved to beat Broome by two and a half lengths in a 1m Group 2 back there a month later.

Form boosted by runner-up Broome, subsequently a neck second to Royal Marine in Group 1 company at Longchamp.

Displayed a smart turn of foot to win both starts, acting well on quick ground. Not sure to stay middle distances but would command great respect if sent over for the 2,000 Guineas. Hard to assess but could potentially prove very smart.

ROYAL MEETING (SAEED BIN SUROOR)

Half-brother by Invincible Spirit to the versatile and tough Heavy Metal out of a winner of a 6f Group 1 in South Africa.

Quickened from off the pace to beat Alrajaa, now rated on 86, in a 7f maiden at Yarmouth in September before taking a marked step up in class to beat Hermosa by three-quarters of a length in the Group 1 7f Criterium International at Chantilly in October.

Stays seven furlongs well but not sure to get beyond a mile. Already a Group 1 winner and likely to remain competitive at that level. Can quicken.

ZAKOUSKI (CHARLIE APPLEBY)

By Shamardal and sixth foal of an unraced sister to Group 1 winners Lonhro and Niello and a half-brother to winners up to 7f.

One of the most impressive maiden winners of the season when sticking his neck out gamely to beat the useful Headman in a 7f novice stakes at Kempton in November, with Rangali Island – now rated on 74 – six and a half lengths behind the winner in third.

Second, previously most impressive at Newcastle, was conceding 7lb and was poorly drawn in stall 12, but form still reads very well.

The winner has every right to take his chance in a Classic trial with a view to stepping up in grade. Not sure to stay beyond a mile but one of the strongest outside chances for the Guineas.

KICK ON (JOHN GOSDEN)

By Charm Spirit and half-brother to seven winners out of a 6f Listed winning daughter of Marju.

Confirmed the promise shown when second in a 7f maiden in August when beating stable companion Humanitarian in a 1m maiden at Newmarket in August. Not disgraced when doing steady late work to finish sixth to Magna Grecia in the Group 1 Vertem Futurity Trophy at Doncaster.

Not bred to stay beyond a mile but certainly runs as if he requires a longer trip. Useful.

PHOENIX OF SPAIN (CHARLIE HILLS)

Lope De Vega seventh foal and a half-brother to six winners including sprinter Lucky Beggar and winners up to 1m 2f. Dam, a daughter of Key Of Luck, is a half-sister to Group winner Special Kaldoun.

Phoenix Of Spain – talented with a turn of foot

Showed the benefit of a tender introduction at Sandown when winning an extended 7f novice stakes at Wolverhampton with a great deal in hand. Followed up next time when coming from last place two furlongs out to get up close home to beat Watan in the Group 3 Acomb Stakes.

Raised again in class for the Group 2 Champagne Stakes at Doncaster, but may have seen too much daylight on the far side when beaten one and three-quarter lengths by Too Darn Hot. Improved again on final start when pipped close home by Magna Grecia in the Group 1 Vertem Futurity Trophy at Doncaster, keeping on well despite being hampered in the final quarter mile.

Already very useful but has the physique to improve and could be a very interesting outsider for the Guineas if he acts on the track. Consistent and travels well. Has the profile to win a big race at a good price.

SANGARIUS (SIR MICHAEL STOUTE)

Kingman fifth foal of a winning half-sister to Group 2 winner Romantica from the family of Dansili and other Group 1 winners including Champs Elysees.

Justified his home reputation when responding gamely to a hands and heels ride to pip Bangkok close home in a 7f novice stakes at Newmarket in August. Still looked green when leading over a furlong out to win the Listed Flying Scotsman Stakes at Doncaster in September. Weak in the market and possibly below his best when fourth next time to Too Darn Hot in the Group 1 Dewhurst Stakes, short of room but not picking up in the final furlong.

Will probably be given a chance to redeem his reputation in a spring trial. Looks held on form but possibly best not judged on his final run.

ALMANIA (SIR MICHAEL STOUTE)

Australia third foal of Group 3-winning daughter of Footstepsinthesand from the family of Group 3 winner Above Average.

Shaped quite well on his Ascot debut in July and built on that next time in a 7f maiden at Sandown, displaying exceptional tenacity to wrestle back the lead off subsequent winner and 89-rated Buffalo River.

Relished the stiff finish at Sandown and likely to appreciate at least a mile, probably further. Has to improve but lacks nothing in courage and likely to earn black type at some point. Very tough.

EPIC HERO (ANDRE FABRE)

Son of Siyouni and second foal of a Group 3-winning half-sister to a bumper and 2m 4f hurdle winner.

Shaped well when third in a 7f contest at Saint-Cloud last June and looked a much improved performer when winning a 1m conditions race at Chantilly in March, still green but hacking up on the bridle. Second, third, fourth and fifth were all previous winners.

Entered for the French Guineas but not the English Guineas, but a name to note wherever he next appears. Looked very special at Chantilly.

AZANO (JOHN GOSDEN)

By Oasis Dream out of a half-sister to Group 1 winner Astarabad from the family of top-class performer Azamour.

Impressed when striding clear to win a 7f novice stakes at Yarmouth in October. Kept on gamely but held in second next time in the Group 3 Horris Hill Stakes.

Likeable sort but needs to improve to prove up to Classic grade.

SKARDU (WILLIAM HAGGAS)

Shamardal first foal of a winning daughter of Iffraaj from the family of a German Group winner.

Caught connections by surprise when coming from a long way back to beat 13 rivals in a 7f maiden at Newmarket in September. Form reads well, with third and fourth subsequently winning and horses now rated in the low 70s finishing in fifth and sixth.

Quickened emphatically to win with something in hand and looks sure to improve. Useful at least.

MAGIC J (ED VAUGHAN)

Not cheap at $950,000 as a yearling out of a US dirt and turf winning miler from a top US family and related to Eclipse winner Hawkbill.

Had shown useful ability at home and justified strong market support when responding to firm hands and heels riding to beat Swindler in a 6f novice stakes at Yarmouth in September. Runner-up and third both now rated on 82.

Has a strong fast-ground bias to his pedigree and not absolutely certain to stay a mile.

CONCLUSION

Too Darn Hot represents the best form but he may lack the scope of a few of his contemporaries and may find the mile on the sharp side.

Of the others Sangarius needs to put his Dewhurst form behind him while Ten Sovereigns may prove best at sprint trips. Magna Grecia could end up being the leading Ballydoyle hope while the unexposed pair Madhmoon and Zakouski command respect.

Jash could be the value to finish in the frame. He ran a top-class race to chase home Ten Sovereigns in the Middle Park and looks the more likely of the two to stay a mile. Next best, for value, are Phoenix Of Spain and Zakouski.

Marten's Telephone Information Line
Established 1980

If you want to keep in touch with Marten's latest thoughts ring him on:

0906 150 1555

Selections given in the first minute
(calls charged at £1.50 a minute at all times)
May cost more from a mobile

A non-premium rate version of this line is available for subscription. Please call the office if you'd like to join our Telephone & Text service.

THE INVESTEC DERBY PREVIEW

Horses listed in order of betting at time of writing.

TOO DARN HOT (JOHN GOSDEN)

Clear head of the pack on two-year-old form but trainer has doubts about his effectiveness over the Derby trip despite grounds for optimism from his pedigree and style of racing.

By Dubawi out of Dar Re Mi, a four-times winner over 1m 4f, twice at Group 1 level, a daughter of Singspiel. Tends to hit a flat spot about a quarter of a mile from home, requires stoking up before striding clear, suggesting that he may be vulnerable over a mile this season.

Seems athletic having proved himself on undulating tracks and likely to be aimed at the Derby if all goes well this spring. Could prove very hard to beat.

JAPAN (AIDAN O'BRIEN)

Cost 1,300,000gns by Galileo and ninth foal of a middle-distance winning half-sister to Arc winner Sagamix. Full brother to Oaks runner-up Secret Gesture and 1m 2f winner Sir Isaac Newton.

Still very green when getting up close home to beat Aristocratic Man in a 7f maiden at Listowel in September, running all over the place from the home turn before knuckling down to assert and win going away by three-quarters of a length.

Again took a while to pick up when beating Mount Everest by a short head in a 1m Group 2 at Naas, responding to pressure throughout the final two furlongs.

Galileo – the leading sire of his generation

Already marked down by his trainer as a middle-distance colt and bred to relish the step up to a mile and a half, if not beyond. Rating of 108 reflects the improvement he needs to find but may bridge the gap when raised in trip. Looks tough.

ANTHONY VAN DYCK (AIDAN O'BRIEN)

Highly regarded son of Galileo half-brother to winners up to 7f from a mainly speedy bottom line.

The winner of three of his seven starts at two and ran notably well when second to Quorto in 7f Group 1 at the Curragh in September and third to Too Darn Hot in the Dewhurst.

A tough colt who is sure to figure at the highest level but not remotely bred on his distaff side to stay middle distances and may be best at a mile, perhaps 1m 2f.

DUBAI WARRIOR (JOHN GOSDEN)

Son of Dansili and full brother to Group 3-winning Mootasadir; third foal of South African Group 1 and UAE Group 2 winner by Galileo.

Very easy well-backed winner of 1m novice contest at Chelmsford in November, with now 77-rated Nabbeyl beaten five lengths in third.

Has plenty to find, having run to a mark in the high 80s through the third, but bred to stay middle distances and apparently rated one of the most promising colts in his powerful yard. One to note for an early trial.

CIRCUS MAXIMUS (AIDAN O'BRIEN)

Galileo first foal of Duntle, a winner of four races including at a mile including the Group 2 Duke of Cambridge Stakes at Royal Ascot, and later placed twice in Group 1 company, again over a mile.

Won a Gowran Park maiden in heavy ground, despite drifting right, before running third to Persian King in Group 3 company at Newmarket. Kept on well when a close fourth to stable companion Magna Grecia in the Group 1 Vertem Futurity Trophy at Doncaster in October.

Clearly talented and acts in soft ground, but currently assessed a few pounds behind the best and not absolutely sure to improve for the step up to middle distances.

BROOME (AIDAN O'BRIEN)

By Australia and sixth foal of a daughter of Acclamation that won up to a mile. Half-brother to 1m 4f winner Horseshoe Bay and two winners at up to a mile.

Kept on well to win an extended 1m maiden at Galway in August before finishing sixth to Phoenix Of Spain in a Group 3 at York and runner-up to the promising Madhmoon in a Group 2 at Leopardstown. Kept on gamely after racing prominently on final outing in a Group 1 at Longchamp in October, beaten a neck by Royal Marine.

Runs as if he should stay beyond a mile but not bred to. Has leeway to make up but the type who could improve enough to figure at a high level.

CONSTANTINOPLE (AIDAN O'BRIEN)

Galileo eighth foal of an unraced sister to Fillies' Mile and Falmouth

Stakes winner Simply Perfect and brother to four winners at up to 1m 6f.

Third in a maiden to Kick On at Newmarket before striding well clear to win a 1m maiden at Thurles in October.

Seemed to be improving fast last autumn and could be one to monitor this spring, especially if placed to run in one of the traditional trials. Should stay middle distances.

HUMANITARIAN (JOHN GOSDEN)

Noble Mission sixth foal of US 1m-winning half-sister to middle-distance winner Pomology and a half-brother to winners at around a mile.

Shaped well despite being green when runner-up to stable companion Kick On in decent 1m maiden at Newmarket in September before pulling clear to beat rivals now rated 82 and 72 in a 1m novice stakes at Lingfield in November.

Useful at least and should stay beyond a mile.

MOUNT EVEREST (AIDAN O'BRIEN)

Galileo ninth foal of triple Group/Grade 1 winner Six Perfections and a full brother to useful middle-distance performers.

Very tough when winning a 1m maiden at the Curragh on his third start and then when pipped close home by stable companion Japan in a Group 2 at Naas in September.

Not far behind the best and entitled to improve more than most for a step up to middle distances. Has a pedigree thick with stamina and may be one to keep in mind for the St Leger and Cup races next year. Likeable.

Sea The Stars – winner of six consecutive Group 1 races as a three-year-old

NORWAY (AIDAN O'BRIEN)

Galileo full brother to Derby winner Ruler Of The World and a half-brother to the top-class Duke Of Marmalade.

Won a 1m maiden at Naas on his third start and then won 1m 2f Listed Zetland Stakes at Newmarket, looking in trouble at halfway but devouring the ground up the hill and staying on well. Fourth of nine on final start in 1m 2f Group 1 Criterium de Saint-Cloud.

Looks an out-and-out stayer with a long-distance programme ahead of him. Lacks gears.

RAKAN (DERMOT WELD)

Sea The Stars first foal of Tarfasha, a dual Group winner and runner-up in the Oaks for this trainer.

Kept on well under strong driving to beat 19 rivals in a 1m maiden at Leopardstown in October, staying on dourly to the line.

Rated a top-class prospect by his handler and should stay the Derby trip. One to keep in mind.

GREAT BEAR (ROGER CHARLTON)

Dansili half-brother to 2m winner Dubhe out of Irish Oaks winner Great Heavens from the family of Nathaniel and Playful Act.

Responded gamely to pressure to beat Copal, now rated on 78, by half a length in an extended 1m novice stakes at Wolverhampton in November.

Ran to a mark in the low 80s and looks the type to work his way up through middle-distance handicaps, perhaps on to better things.

A FEW OTHERS...

Alfaatik (Gosden) By Sea The Stars and related to a middle-distance winner, overcame greenness to win a 1m 2f novice stakes at Chelmsford in December.

Apparate (Varian) By Dubawi out of an unraced daughter of Galileo related to Flintshire and Enable, took a while to pick up before running on strongly to finish second to Landa Beach in a 1m novice stakes at Newbury in October. He is bred to stay very well and ran accordingly.

Baltic Song (Gosden) By Sea The Stars out of a winning 1m 6f daughter of Sadler's Wells, quickened well to win a 1m 4f novice stakes at Lingfield in February. He looks destined to work his way through the handicap ranks.

Bangkok (Balding) By Australia out of a Darshaan mare, is bred to stay well. Rated 88 after three fair efforts, including against Sangarius and Kick On, he is one to keep in mind for staying handicaps. Won at Doncaster in March.

El Misk (Gosden) A son of Dansili out of a daughter of Galileo. The dam won at a mile and a half and he will stay well.

First In Line (Gosden) An unraced son of New Approach from the family of top middle-distance performers including Our Obsession and Golden Horn.

Fox Tai (Balding) By Sea The Stars from the family of Luso, is rated 109 having ended the season with a one-length second in the Criterium de Saint-Cloud. He should prove effective in staying races just below the top level.

Ginistrelli (Walker) By Frankel out of a middle-distance winning half-sister to Fame And Glory, kept on well to beat 83-rated James Park Woods in a 1m novice stakes at Newmarket in October. Connections have hopes for him. One to note.

Invictus Spirit (Stoute) An unraced son of Frankel and the ninth foal of a 1m 4f-winning half-sister to Oaks runner-up Flight Of Fancy. His trainer does not make frivolous entries.

Landa Beach (Balding) Kept on well to beat the promising Apparate by a neck in a 1m novice stakes at Newbury in October. By Teofilo out of an unraced half-sister to a 1m Group 2 winner.

Logician (Gosden) An unraced son of Frankel out of a half-sister to Group 1 winner Cityscape. Bred to stay well.

Makmour (Rouget) By Rock Of Gibraltar from a family of strong stayers. The winner of his first start at Deauville in November, he finished second to Starmaniac at Saint-Cloud in March when stepped up in trip to an extended 1m 2f. He is probably useful.

Mubariz (Charlton) Made all to win his third start over an extended mile at Nottingham, eased down, in October. Carried his head high but won with great authority having shaped well in the good maiden won by Kick On at Newmarket. Should prove effective off 89 before progressing to better things.

Questionare (Gosden) Got up close home to win an extended 1m 1f novice stakes at Wolverhampton in March. Runner-up rated 72 but by Galileo out of a Dansili mare so he will stay well.

Surfman (Varian) Shaped well to beat Durston in an extended 1m maiden at Nottingham in November, striding clear inside the final furlong. Well thought of by his trainer, he is a half-brother to Group 1 middle-distance winner Kitesurf from a good staying family. Useful.

Swift Wing (Gosden) An unraced son of Pivotal and a full brother to Eagle Top and Wings Of Desire. From a very good staying family he is one for the longer term.

Sydney Opera House (Aidan O'Brien) Finished behind Madhmoon, Mohawk and Norway in three outings last season before running the winner to a neck in the 1m 2f Group 1 Criterium de Saint-Cloud.

Tankerville (Weld) Needed just gentle encouragement to go and win a 1m maiden at Gowran Park in October. The third, beaten just over three lengths, is now rated on 79. By Kitten's Joy and the dam won over a mile and a half. Well regarded.

Waldstern (Gosden) Rated 98, could be on the verge of Group class. Runner-up to the useful Kadar at Haydock he was then fourth to Norway in the 1m 2f Zetland Stakes at Newmarket. By Sea The Stars out of a Monsun mare he is from the family of St Leger winner Masked Marvel and is bred to stay extreme distances. A likely Cup horse.

Wirraway (Gosden) An unraced son of Australia out of a half-sister to a 1m 7f Listed winner by Zamindar. His trainer rates him quite highly.

Zuba (Perrett) Took two starts before winning a 1m 2f maiden at Chelmsford in October, with a 71-rated colt back in third. Most unlikely to be Group class but was progressing nicely last season. Bred to stay well.

Zuenoon (Weld) Battled on dourly to beat Cardini, who ran well against Too Darn Hot at Doncaster, at Killarney in August. By Havana Gold out of a well-related unraced daughter of Dalakhani so should stay beyond a mile. Tough.

CONCLUSION

There are many lightly raced or even unraced colts with the potential to make the grade if Too Darn Hot should fall by the wayside or be deemed a doubtful stayer.

Aidan O'Brien has a plethora of entries, with Japan and Mount Everest looking two of the more likely candidates. Of the others, once-raced colts Dubai Warrior and Rakan are worth noting in early trials.

I hope to see Too Darn Hot earn the right to try the trip. Japan and Dubai Warrior are also interesting.

THE QIPCO 1,000 GUINEAS PREVIEW

Horses listed in order of betting at time of writing.

JUST WONDERFUL (AIDAN O'BRIEN)

By Dansili and a half-sister to sprint winner Lost Treasure. Dam is a half-sister to Irish Oaks winner Bracelet from the family of Sea The Stars and Galileo.

Very experienced, having raced seven times at two, notably beating the strong-finishing Dandhu in the Group 2 Rockfel Stakes, travelling well and quickening away to win by one and three-quarter lengths.

Lost her chance at the start when not disgraced in fourth on her final start in the Breeders' Cup Juvenile Fillies Turf at Churchill Downs.

Very highly regarded by her trainer and jockey Ryan Moore but may not like to hit the front too soon. Already proven over a mile and bred to stay middle distances.

FAIRYLAND (AIDAN O'BRIEN)

Kodiac filly out of an unraced half-sister to Group 1 winner Dream Ahead by Pivotal.

Got up close home to win Group 1 Cheveley Park Stakes on her final start having won three of her earlier four starts, only defeat coming when unlucky third of 18 to Main Edition in the Group 3 Albany Stakes at Royal Ascot, racing clear and finishing in front on the far side.

Not devoid of speed and looked very game when winning the Lowther Stakes at York, but there must be a doubt about her staying a mile, although she relaxes well and will probably be aimed at this race.

SKITTER SCATTER (JOHN OXX)

By Scat Daddy and a half-sister to US Graded Stakes-placed 1m turf winner out of 1m 2f winning daughter of Street Cry from the family of Group 1 winner Intense Focus.

Kept busy last season, running seven times and winning four, notably displaying great tenacity to win her last three starts in a Group 3, a Group 2 and finally the Group 1 Moyglare Stud Stakes at the Curragh, staying on strongly to assert inside the final furlong. Line through runner-up Lady Kaya leaves her a couple of pounds behind Cheveley Park winner Fairyland.

Skitter Scatter – blessed with an admirable temperament to match her ability

Has progressed with each race and although untried beyond seven furlongs runs as if she will stay a mile. Tries very hard and blessed with an admirable temperament. Never been out of the first three and cannot be discounted if she stays the mile. Immensely likeable.

DANCING VEGA (RALPH BECKETT)

By Lope De Vega and fourth foal of New Zealand dual Group 1 winner by Starcraft, half-sister to two winners up to 1m 2f.

Hugely impressive to the eye when sauntering clear, despite racing keenly throughout, to beat 78-rated Blue Gardenia in a 1m maiden fillies' contest at Doncaster in October, with another 78-rated rival back in third.

Ratings of second and third temper enthusiasm for the value of the form, but won with loads in hand and clearly very useful. Hard to assess and more will be known after a trial. May stay beyond a mile.

IRIDESSA (JOSEPH O'BRIEN)

By Derby winner Ruler Of The World out of an unraced half-sister to middle-distance winner Media Stars from the family of a Breeders' Cup winner.

Well held by Skitter Scatter in a 7f Group 2 at the Curragh in August and then ran a creditable third in 7f Listed race at Leopardstown before coming through rivals to beat Hermosa in the Fillies' Mile at Newmarket.

Thought more likely to make an Oaks filly but entitled to take her chance in the Guineas. Stays well.

EAST (KEVIN RYAN)

Daughter of Frankel and a full sister to 1m winner Golden Hooves from the family of Cheveley Park winner Pass The Peace.

Followed up 6f debut win at Hamilton with defeat of Pretty Boy in a 7f Group 3 at Saint-Cloud in October. Shaped very well when distant runner-up to Newspaperofrecord in Grade 1 Breeders' Cup Juvenile Fillies Turf next time at Churchill Downs.

Stays the mile well but hard to assess in relation to her contemporaries.

HERMOSA (AIDAN O'BRIEN)

Galileo full sister to Group 1 middle-distance winner Hydrangea from the family of Group class sprinters.

Won two of her seven starts but showed best form when placed in three Group 1 contests, third to Skitter Scatter at the Curragh in September and runner-up to Iridessa in the Fillies' Mile and to Royal Meeting in the Group 1 Criterium International at Chantilly.

Has form that ties her in with the best of her generation but needs to find a few pounds to beat them.

PRETTY POLLYANNA (MICHAEL BELL)

By Oasis Dream out of an unraced daughter of Shamardal and a half-sister to US 1m 1f Grade 3 winner from the family of User Friendly.

Made a winning debut at Yarmouth and not disgraced when fifth in the Albany Stakes before winning the 6f Group 2 Duchess Of Cambridge Stakes by seven lengths and the Group 1 Prix Morny from Signora Cabello. Again shaped well when fourth to Fairyland in the Cheveley Park and third to Iridessa in the Fillies' Mile.

Seemed to stay the mile well enough on her final start and ties in with the best of her generation's form. May lack the scope of a few of her contemporaries.

SO PERFECT (AIDAN O'BRIEN)

Daughter of Scat Daddy out of a speedy half-sister to a 1m 1f Grade 2 winner by Songandaprayer.

Won two of her first four starts but showed her best form when half-length second to Advertise in the Group 1 Phoenix Stakes and third to Fairyland in the Cheveley Park Stakes at Newmarket.

Gutsy sort but seems held by others and not sure to stay a mile.

FASHION'S STAR (ROGER CHARLTON)

Sea The Stars first foal of a half-sister to middle-distance Group 1 winner in Hong Kong from the family of a German Oaks winner.

Cosy winner of a 7f Class 2 contest at Newbury from Roxy Art, now rated on 87.

Evidently has potential but lacks experience and looks a more likely Oaks contender.

ANGEL'S HIDEAWAY (JOHN GOSDEN)

Daughter of Dark Angel and full sister to winners over 6f out of a 5f-winning daughter of Kheleyf from the family of an Oaks third.

Performed to a consistent level in Group-class company but well held by Fairyland at York and Newmarket and runner-up in Group 3 on her final start.

Looks held on form and far from certain to stay a mile.

DANDHU (DAVID ELSWORTH)

By Dandy Man and half-sister to winners up to 1m 2f out of an unraced half-sister to 1m Group 1 winner Rajeem from the family of Hoh Magic.

Showed steadily progressive form winning a 7f Class 2 at Kempton on her third start before improving significantly to chase home Just Wonderful in the Group 2 Rockfel Stakes, staying on strongly from off the pace to finish full of running.

Shaped as if she would suit a mile on her final start and very well regarded by her trainer. Acts on quick ground and may have more scope than some of those ahead of her in the market. The type to run into the frame at long odds.

A FEW OTHERS...

Chaleur (Beckett) By Dansili and fair third to Pretty Pollyanna in Duchess Of Cambridge Stakes before proving well treated off a mark of 89 in a 7f nursery in September. Likely to be earning black type at some point.

Clematis (Hills) Impressive winner of a 1m novice stakes at Kempton in November, well backed beforehand and hanging fire for a few strides before finding a turn of foot to go three lengths clear of now 77-rated runner up. By First Defence and half-sister to a winner up to 1m 6f. Hard to assess but looked useful at Kempton and should have scope to progress.

Clerisy (Stoute) Daughter of Kingman and a half-sister to Breeders' Cup Turf winner Expert Eye from the family of Cheveley Park and 1,000 Guineas winner Special Duty. Shaped in encouraging fashion when tenderly handled third on her debut in a 7f novice stakes at Wolverhampton in December. Lowly beginnings but would not be entered for this race if her trainer did not rate her worthy of it.

Fire Fly (Aidan O'Brien) Daughter of Galileo and was making good progress last season, winning a maiden at Tipperary in August, but was slowly away in the 1,000 Guineas Trial at Leopardstown in April and finished down the field.

Fleeting (Aidan O'Brien) By Zoffany and won the 1m Group 2 May Hill Stakes at Doncaster having run third to Just Wonderful in a 1m Group 3 at the Curragh earlier in the month. Dam won up to 1m 6f so one to keep in mind for middle-distance races this summer. Probably capable of being placed at Group 1 level and worth keeping an eye on.

Frosty (Aidan O'Brien) Full sister to English and Irish Guineas winner Winter out of useful Wokingham Stakes winner Laddies Poker Two. Green when winning 7f maiden at Dundalk in September before disappointing when last but one to Mot Juste in Group 3 Oh So Sharp Stakes at Newmarket. Entitled to improve.

Garrel Glen (Tompkins) By Mount Nelson and a half-sister to a winner up to 2m out of a dam from the family of Clumber Place and US Grade 1 winner Bequest. Very pleasing winner of 7f novice auction stakes at Newmarket in October, with 77-rated rival in second. Form only modest by these standards but this is a decent sort with the potential to earn black type.

Imperial Charm (Crisford) Half-sister to four winners at up to 1m 4f out of a daughter of Mark Of Esteem that won over 1m 2f. Did well given her breeding to win a 7f novice stakes at Newmarket on her third start, appreciating the ease underfoot. Well regarded and entitled to find considerable improvement when stepped up to middle distances.

Kiss For A Jewel (Weld) Promising maiden daughter of Kingman, second foal of useful 1m 4f winner Sapphire, who ran a useful second to Delphinia – now rated 91 – at Galway in October. Probably fairly useful but may require middle distances to realise her potential.

Lady Lawyer (Gosden) Daughter of Blame out of a winning daughter of War Front, ran out a cosy winner of a 7f novice stakes at Kempton in October. Form put in perspective by proximity of a 72-rated filly in third but probably useful with scope to improve.

Magic Fountain (Aidan O'Brien) Unraced daughter of War Front out of Irish Oaks winner Bracelet from the family of Sea The Stars and Galileo.

Main Edition (Johnston) Winner of four of her seven starts but beaten by Pretty Pollyanna at Newmarket in July and Skitter Scatter and Just Wonderful on her final two starts of the season. Should stay a mile but needs to make marked improvement.

Modern Millie (Channon) Full sister by Sixties Icon to Epsom Icon from a speedy bottom line. Made a winning debut in a 6f median auction stakes, looking to require every yard of the six furlongs. Well regarded at home.

Mot Juste (Varian) Dam by Sadler's Wells and looks sure to get a mile having made steady progress last season, beating Angel's Hideaway on her final start in a 7f Group 3 at Newmarket. One to note when stepped up beyond a mile.

Muchly (Gosden) Iffraaj half-sister to eight winners all around 7f but just got the mile when beating Lady Adelaide by a neck in a 1m novice stakes at Newbury in October. May be best at trips short of a mile.

Nausha (Varian) Took keen hold before finding sufficient to beat 81-rated Spanish Aria in 1m novice stakes at Newbury in October. By Kingman out of a Galileo mare so should stay beyond a mile if she settles. Promising.

Qabala (Varian) Scat Daddy half-sister to winners up to 9f out of a daughter of Empire Maker, held on well to beat Desirous in a 7f maiden at Newmarket in September. Runner-up won next time now rated 82 and third and fourth also won, with others running with credit, so form reads well. Useful.

Queen Power (Stoute) Well related daughter of Shamardal who made hard work of beating subsequent winner Duneflower in 7f maiden at Newmarket in October. Had shown ability at home for former trainer Ralph Beckett. Needs to make vast improvement but may do under her current trainer.

Secret Thoughts (Aidan O'Brien) By War Front and the first foal of Irish Oaks winner Chicquita. Did very well to win her second start over 6f given her stout pedigree and improved when third to Skitter Scatter on her next start in 7f Group 3 contest at Leopardstown. The type to progress, especially when stepped up in trip.

Star Terms (Hannon) Sea The Stars filly out of speedy daughter of Exceed And Excel from the family of Time Charter. Progressed from winning a 7f nursery at Newmarket off 83 to running second in Group 2 May Hill Stakes and third, beaten a neck when short of room, in Group 1 Prix Marcel Boussac in October. Improved by an official margin of 25lb in her last two runs and being trained for the Guineas. Not without a chance.

Suphala (Fabre) Daughter of Frankel from the family of useful performer Pursuit Of Glory, in turn from the family of top-class Serena's Song. Won her second and third starts over a mile at Chantilly in September. Hard to assess but evidently well regarded by her handler.

Watheerah (Burrows) Daughter of Dubawi who confirmed the promise shown when a short-head second of 12 on her debut in a 7f maiden at Newmarket in October when quickening to beat 84-rated Al Mureib in a 7f maiden at Kempton in November. From the family of 1,000 Guineas winner Ghanaati and from a family mainly of milers. Looked useful at Kempton and likely to earn black type at some point.

CONCLUSION

Just Wonderful and Skitter Scatter make most appeal of the market leaders, but I expect improvement from Dandhu, Star Terms and we need to keep an eye on the unexposed Clerisy.

Others that may emerge from spring trials are Fleeting and Imperial Charm. Let's stick with Just Wonderful and Skitter Scatter.

Marten's Telephone Information Line
Established 1980

If you want to keep in touch with Marten's latest
thoughts ring him on:

0906 150 1555

Selections given in the first minute
(calls charged at £1.50 a minute at all times)
May cost more from a mobile

A non-premium rate version of this line is available for subscription.
Please call the office if you'd like to join our Telephone & Text service.

THE INVESTEC OAKS PREVIEW

No entries were available for this race at the time of writing. Horses listed in order of betting at time of writing.

Iridessa (Joseph O'Brien) By Derby winner Ruler Of The World out of an unraced half-sister to a middle-distance winner. She won the Group 1 Fillies' Mile in dour fashion last season and should stay the trip.

Just Wonderful (Aidan O'Brien) Had two ways of running last season but at her best she looked very good, notably when quickening to beat the promising Dandhu by one and three-quarter lengths in the Group 2 Rockfel Stakes. By Dansili out of a full sister to Irish Oaks winner Bracelet from the family of Sea The Stars and Galileo, so confidently expected to improve over middle distances.

Just Wonderful – has the talent to win at the highest level

Hermosa (Aidan O'Brien) Runner-up to Iridessa at Newmarket and to Royal Meeting at Chantilly. Full sister to Group 1 middle-distance winner Hydrangea from a speedy bottom line. Not entirely certain to stay a mile and a half.

Chablis (Aidan O'Brien) Stayed on strongly to beat Peruvian Lily in 7f maiden at Gowran Park in October. Cost 1,500,000gns as a yearling and full sister to The Pentagon out of a middle-distance winning daughter of Unfuwain. Runner-up rated on 83. Bred to thrive over a mile and a half and could prove very decent.

Manuela De Vega (Ralph Beckett) Looked an out-and-out stayer when finding plenty off the bridle to win 7f maiden at Salisbury and 1m Listed race at Pontefract, on second occasion beating 95-rated runner, conceding 5lb, in second. Full sister to 1m 4f winner Isabel De Urbina out of a Listed-placed daughter of Daylami. Sure to relish a distance of ground and looks very tough.

Goddess (Aidan O'Brien) Very easy winner of 7f maiden on her second start before finishing last of six when odds-on to win a 7f Group 3 at Leopardstown in July. Not seen thereafter. By Camelot out of a winning mare related to Sea The Stars but not absolutely certain to stay the Oaks trip.

Dancing Vega (Ralph Beckett) Most impressive to the eye when quickening on the bridle to beat 78-rated Blue Gardenia in 1m maiden at Doncaster in October. By Lope De Vega and half-sister to winners over 1m 2f but needs to settle better if she is to excel over middle distances. Needs to improve but may do so.

Fleeting (Aidan O'Brien) Daughter of Zoffany who steadily improved last season, staying on well to beat Star Terms in 1m Group 2 at Doncaster in September. Looked a potential stayer in her manner of winning and should have the class to prove competitive at middle distances.

Rainbow Heart (William Haggas) Daughter of Born To Sea who drew eight lengths clear of subsequent winner Pytilia in a 7f median auction stakes at Newmarket in October. Runner-up now rated on 77 but won in the most authoritative fashion. Dam won over 1m 3f and from the family of Yorkshire Oaks winner Sarah Siddons.

Fashion's Star (Roger Charlton) Very cosy winner of 7f conditions stakes at Newbury from now 87-rated Roxy Art. Won with plenty in hand having shown talent in her work at home. By Dutch Art and first foal of Group-placed half-sister to winners at up to a mile, so not absolutely sure to stay a mile and a half.

Chaleur (Ralph Beckett) Well treated when winning a 7f nursery off 89 at Newmarket in September, now rated on 98. By Dansili out of a daughter of First Defence related to winners up to 1m 2f. May stay a mile and a half.

Dandhu (David Elsworth) By sprinter Dandy Man out of a half-sister to winners up to 1m 2f and shaped as if she would get further when staying on strongly to chase home Just Wonderful in 7f Group 2 at Newmarket in September. By no means certain to get the Oaks trip but looks talented and may defy her pedigree.

Frankellina (William Haggas) First foal of 1m 4f-winning daughter of Shamardal from the family of Rebecca Sharp and Golden Horn. Got up close home to win 1m novice stakes at Yarmouth in October. Very well bred and entitled to stay beyond a mile, probably a mile and a half.

Nefertiti (Sir Michael Stoute) Unraced daughter of Galileo out of French 1,000 Guineas and French Oaks winner Divine Proportions. Half-sister to winners up to a mile. Bred to be very useful and has apparently shown talent in her work at home.

Clematis (Charlie Hills) Took a while to find her stride before pulling clear to win a 1m novice stakes at Kempton in November by three lengths. Half-sister to 1m 6f winner Sepal so should stay the Oaks trip.

Garrel Glen (Mark Tompkins) Beat a 77-rated rival on her second start in a 7f median auction stakes at Newmarket and a half-sister to Bracken Brae, a winner up to two miles. Likely to run with credit in decent company at long odds, especially over a mile and more.

Imperial Charm (Simon Crisford) All out when beating Jadeerah in a 7f novice event at Newmarket in November. Half-sister to winners up to 1m 4f including Group 1 winner Ajman Princess. Dam from the family of Afsare. Rated 86 at the moment but expected to improve significantly when stepped up to middle distances. Interesting.

Mot Juste (Roger Varian) Won extended 7f novice stakes at Beverley on her third start and then a Group 2 in October over the same trip. Half-sister to winners up to 1m 4f out of Group 2 middle-distance winner by Sadler's Wells from the family of Time Charter. Looked very game at Newmarket and entitled to stay beyond a mile.

Nausha (Roger Varian) Was keen when beating 81-rated rival in 1m novice stakes at Newbury in October. Related to milers and not sure to stay middle distances, especially if she doesn't settle better.

Secret Thoughts (Aidan O'Brien) By War Front out of Irish Oaks winner Chicquita. Not one of the highly rated horses in her powerful yard but has a solid middle-distance pedigree and showed enough when third to Skitter Scatter in Group 3 company over 7f that she is useful. One to keep an eye on.

CONCLUSION

Just Wonderful, Chablis and Fleeting are serious contenders for Aidan O'Brien. Ralph Beckett has his usual strong hand, with the tough Manuela De Vega of serious interest. Imperial Charm warrants a mention given her stout pedigree.

Just Wonderful and Chablis are the two at this stage.

INDEX

Advertise 53, 54, 77
Al Battar 17
Alfaatik 70
All Points West 7
Almania 7-8, 60
Angel's Hideaway 77, 80
Anthony Van Dyck 52, 55, 65
Apparate 70
Autonomy 39
Azano 60-61
Azwah 18
Babbo's Boy 40
Baltic Song 70
Bangkok 59, 70
Broome 56, 66
Calyx 53, 54
Chablis 18, 84, 86
Chaleur 78, 85
Chancer 8-9
Circus Maximus 66
Clematis 78, 85
Clerisy 78, 82
Constantinople 66-67
Craneur 40-41
Dalaalaat 41-42
Dame Malliot 19
Dancing Vega 75, 84
Dandhu 73, 78, 82, 83, 85
Dubai Warrior 65, 72
Earl Of Harrow 42
East 76
Ebbraam 19
El Misk 70
Eligible 20
Epic Hero 60
Even Keel 9
Fairyland 73-74, 76, 77
Fashion's Star 20-21, 77, 85
Faylaq 21

Fire Fly 79
First In Line 22, 70
Fleeting 79, 82, 84, 86
Fox Tai 70
Frankellina 85
Franz Kafka 22-23
Frosty 79
Garrel Glen 79, 86
Ginistrelli 70
Goddess 84
Great Bear 42-43, 69
Great Midge 10
Grenadier Guard 23
Hermosa 57, 75, 76, 84
Highland Sky 43
Humanitarian 23-24, 58, 67
Imperial Charm 24-25, 79, 82, 86
Invictus Spirit 25, 71
Iridessa 75, 76, 83, 84
Japan 63-64, 67, 72
Jash 52, 55, 62
Jubiloso 26
Just Wonderful 73, 78, 79, 80, 82, 83, 85, 86
Kadar 10-11, 72
Kick On 58, 67, 70, 71
Kiss For A Jewel 26-27, 79
Lady Bowthorpe 44
Lady Lawyer 80
Landa Beach 70, 71
Line Of Duty 56
Loch Laggan 27
Logician 27, 71
Madhmoon 56, 62, 66, 71
Magic Fountain 80
Magic J 28-29, 61
Magna Grecia 53, 54, 58, 59, 62, 66
Main Edition 73, 80
Makmour 71

Mannguy 29
Manuela De Vega 84, 86
Matchmaking 11-12
Mawsoof 29
Mia Maria 30
Millers Creek 44-45
Modern Millie 80
Mot Juste 79, 80, 86
Mount Everest 63, 67, 72
Mubariz 71
Muchly 80
Name The Wind 30-31
Nantucket 31
Nausha 80, 86
Nefertiti 85
Norway 69, 71, 72
Our Oystercatcher 45
Paseo 32
Pearl Of Manama 32
Persian King 53, 54, 66
Phoenix Of Spain 53, 58-59, 62, 66
Play It By Ear 12
Pretty Pollyanna 76-77, 78, 80
Qabala 80-81
Queen Guanhumara 33-34
Queen Power 81
Questionare 71
Quorto 51-52, 55, 65
Rainbow Heart 34, 85
Rakan 69, 72
Road To Paris 45-46
Royal Marine 56, 66

Royal Meeting 57, 76, 84
Sangarius 59, 62, 70
Secret Thoughts 81, 86
Set Piece 15, 35
Shareef Star 12-13
Silent Hunter 36
Skardu 61
Skitter Scatter 74-75, 76, 80, 81, 82, 86
So Perfect 77
Socru 46-47
Sovereign Grant 14
Sparkle In His Eye 14-15, 35
Star Terms 81, 82, 84
Suphala 81
Surfman 36-37, 71
Swift Wing 37-38, 71
Sydney Opera House 56, 71
Tabdeed 15-16
Tankerville 72
Ten Sovereigns 52, 55, 62
Thanks Be 47
Too Darn Hot 50, 51, 52, 53, 54, 55, 59, 61, 63, 65, 72
Venture 48
Waldstern 11, 72
Watheerah 81-82
Wings Of Time 38
Wirraway 72
Zakouski 57, 62
Zuba 48-49, 72
Zuenoon 72